Borderline
Personality

The GOSPEL for REAL LIFE series

Brad Hambrick, Series Editor

Borderline Personality

A SCRIPTURAL PERSPECTIVE

CATHY WISEMAN

P&R
PUBLISHING
P.O. BOX 817 • PHILLIPSBURG • NEW JERSEY 08865-0817

Unless otherwise indicated, Scripture quotations are from The Holy Bible, New King James Version. Copyright © 1979, 1980, 1982, Thomas Nelson, Inc.

Scripture quotations marked (MSG) are taken from *The Message*. Copyright © 1993, 1994, 1995, 1996, 2000, 2001, 2002. Used by permission of NavPress publishing group.

Scripture quotations marked (NIV) are from the HOLY BIBLE, NEW INTERNATIONAL VERSION®. NIV®. Copyright © 1973, 1978, 1984 by International Bible Society. Used by permission of Zondervan Publishing House. All rights reserved.

Italics within Scripture quotations indicate emphasis added.

Printed in the United States of America

Library of Congress Cataloging-in-Publication Data

Wiseman, Cathy, 1943-
  Borderline personality : a scriptural perspective / Cathy Wiseman.
    p. cm. -- (The Gospel for real life)
  Includes bibliographical references.
  ISBN 978-1-59638-422-4 (pbk.)
  1. Borderline personality disorder. 2. Christian women--Religious life.
I. Title.
  RC569.5.B67W575 2012
  616.85'852--dc23
                            2012006691

For several years, I worked for a psychiatrist who specialized in borderline personality disorder (BPD), and I counseled many with this disorder. Although I was a Christian, I did not understand how Christ could make a profound difference to BPD persons, even if they were Christians themselves. Why not? Because I believed the psychiatric literature, which taught me that they had to go through years of therapy before they could emotionally and cognitively grasp reality. I hoped those necessary years of therapy would bring them to the place where they could cognitively understand spiritual truths. For years I anxiously waited, prayed, and hoped they would come to believe, understand, and live by the ultimate reality of God's Word. But that hope never came true.

Although I learned about BPD in graduate school, it was very different to actually work with those who suffered from it. Their sense of despair was palpable as they desperately tried to connect with (actually consume) someone who would not abandon them. Even perceived abandonment sent them spiraling into suicidal depression or extreme rage. I very much wanted to help them out of their deep despair.

So I read all the research and tried every therapy the experts prescribed. I was available 24/7, and I prayed with all my heart for their healing while the psychiatrist prescribed cocktails of medication. But nothing we did could fill their agonizing emptiness. After several years, I reached the end of my rope, totally exhausted from working with those suffering with BPD. God brought me to the end of myself by graciously showing me how utterly incapable I was to do something that only he can do and how foolish I had been to depend on psychiatric theories to cure *his* children.

I began to trust God's wisdom to heal those with this diagnosis rather than to depend on psychological theories with portions of Scripture tacked on. Christians who struggled with BPD now learned that they were actually battling with the flesh and needed to learn to trust God and begin to walk in the Spirit. Easy? No. Magic? No. Change happened the same way it happens for all Christians—through spiritual battle: "the blood, sweat, and tears of dying to self and listening to God."[1] They "put off" their "issue-based identity" (BPD) and "put on" (Eph. 4:22–24) their "Christ-identity."[2] With that identity in place and supported by brothers and sisters in Christ, they began to grasp the truth of the gospel: they had died with Christ and were therefore "no longer . . . slaves of sin" (Rom. 6:6)—or of BPD!

DEFINITIONS OF BPD

Psychological Definition

The Diagnostic and Statistical Manual of the American Psychiatric Association, Edition IV (DSM-IV) describes BPD as follows:

> a pervasive pattern of instability of interpersonal relationships, self-image, and affects [emotions], and marked impulsivity beginning by early adulthood and present in a variety of contexts, as indicated by five (or more) of the following [nine symptoms: identity disturbance/unstable sense of self; chronic feelings of emptiness; fear of abandonment; emotional instability; unstable interpersonal relationships; intense rage; paranoia or dissociative symptoms; impulsivity/self-damaging behaviors; suicidal/self-mutilating behavior].[3]

1. David Powlison, *Power Encounters: Reclaiming Spiritual Warfare* (Grand Rapids: Baker, 1995), 119.

2. Mike Wilkerson, *Redemption: Freed by Jesus from the Idols We Worship and the Wounds We Carry* (Wheaton, IL: Crossway, 2011), 16.

3. *The Diagnostic and Statistical Manual of the American Psychiatric Association, Edition IV* (Washington, DC: American Psychological Association, 1994), 280.

These nine symptoms from the *DSM-IV* will be discussed more fully later in this booklet.

Biblical Definition

Now compare the definition above to this biblical one, which describes people with BPD as having

> a pervasive pattern of demanding interpersonal relationships, unstable self-image, volatile emotions, and marked impulsiveness. These individuals demand suffocating intimacy in their relationships and yet their hurtful behavior destroys those same relationships.[4]

Just as the *DSM-IV* uses symptoms to define BPD, the Bible also defines the BPD-type symptoms (or behaviors) mentioned above as "works of the flesh" that originate in the heart. Although the biblical description may at first sound cruel to BPD sufferers, it is actually good news, because Christ died to save us from these kinds of sinful behaviors:

> Now the works of the flesh are evident, which are: adultery, fornication, uncleanness, lewdness, idolatry, sorcery, hatred, contentions, jealousies, outbursts of wrath, selfish ambitions, dissensions, heresies, envy, murders, drunkenness, revelries, and the like . . . (Gal. 5:19–21)

Listen to the same verses from *The Message*:

> It is obvious what kind of life develops out of trying to get your own way all the time: repetitive, loveless, cheap sex; a stinking accumulation of mental and emotional garbage; frenzied and joyless grabs for happiness; trinket gods; magic-show religion; paranoid loneliness, cutthroat competition; all-consuming-yet-

4. Marshall Asher and Mary Asher, *The Christian's Guide to Psychological Terms* (Bemidji, MN: Focus, 2004), 27.

never-satisfied wants; a brutal temper; an impotence to love or be loved; divided homes and divided lives; small-minded and lopsided pursuits; the vicious habit of depersonalizing everyone into a rival; uncontrolled and uncontrollable addictions; ugly parodies of community.

Also, those labeled with BPD are unstable because they are emotionally and spiritually immature, and those problems are also addressed by Scripture:

When I was a child, I spoke as a child, I understood as a child, I thought as a child; but when I became a man, I put away childish things. (1 Cor. 13:11)

We should no longer be children, tossed to and fro and carried about with every wind of doctrine . . . (Eph. 4:14)

For he who doubts is like a wave of the sea driven and tossed by the wind. . . . He is a double-minded man, unstable in all his ways. (James 1:6, 8)

A commentary on James 1:8 teaches: "Double-minded is literally 'two souls.' If one part of a person is set on God and the other is set on this world, there will be constant conflict within."[5]

THE CAUSE OF BPD

Psychological Theories

Although the DSM-IV describes the symptoms of BPD, it does not give its cause. No psychological causes for BPD have been proven, though there are many theories—a majority of

5. Earl D. Radmacher, Ronald B. Allen, and H. Wayne House, eds., *The Nelson Study Bible* (Nashville: Thomas Nelson, 1997), 2105.

which are based on the experience of child abuse in people with BPD. However,

> not all studies have found a high rate of child abuse in border-line personalities. And there is a risk of reinforcing distorted memories in people who are already inclined to justifying their own behavior by denouncing others. Most experts believe that although child abuse and other traumatic events may have some influence on borderline symptoms, these experiences are not usually the cause of the disorder.[6]

Object relations theory has long been regarded as a predominant cause of BPD. The theory posits that a toddler must learn that his mother (or *object*) will consistently be available for emotional refueling, proving that he can leave and come back to her without fear of abandonment. The mother's consistency (*object constancy*) helps the toddler to learn "improved reality perception; frustration tolerance; and impulse control . . . [and] the capacity to be alone, to tolerate anxiety and depression, to show concern and feel guilt" (which BPD persons seemingly cannot do).[7] The theory's bottom line is that BPD is caused if the child does not develop object constancy because the mother did not provide it.

Newer research on BPD, using

> evidence from functional magnetic resonance imaging showing that patients with BPD have *hyperactivity* in the limbic areas of the brain, especially the amygdala, and *hypoactivity* in the prefrontal cortex [and] in complex interaction with childhood trauma common among borderline patients, can result in the . . . behavior recognized as the symptoms of BPD:

6. Michael Miller, "Borderline Personality Disorder: Origins and Symptoms," *Harvard Mental Health Letter* 22, no. 12 (2006): 1–3.

7. James F. Masterson, *Psychotherapy of the Borderline Adult: A Developmental Approach* (New York: Brunner/Mazel, 1976), 32–33.

impulsive aggression, lack of affective control, and a profound mistrust born out of early disruption in the development of emotional attachment.[8]   .

Obviously, psychological theories for BPD focus on different causes: child abuse; the inability to attach; genetics; neurobiology; or a combination of all. Yet "there is some kind of core to borderline pathology that is not about being either impulsive or emotional or interpersonally sensitive, something that isn't wholly captured by any of these characteristics."[9]

Biblical Cause (Not Theory)

God says that "the core" of BPD, just like the core of every other so-called personality disorder, is "motivated by our core commitments, our basic beliefs—what the Bible terms 'the heart' and describes as the center of our being."[10]

> But those things which proceed out of the mouth come from the heart, and they defile a man. For out of the heart proceed evil thoughts, murders, adulteries, fornications, thefts, false witness, blasphemies. These are the things which defile a man . . . (Matt. 15:18–20)

> What comes out of a man, that defiles a man. For from within, out of the heart of men, proceed evil thoughts, adulteries, fornications, murders, thefts, covetousness, wickedness, deceit, lewdness, an evil eye, blasphemy, pride, foolishness. All these evil things come from within and defile a man. (Mark 7:20–23)

8. Mark Moran, "Gabbard Weds Neurobiology Psychodynamics in BPD Treatment," *Psychiatric News* 46, no. 7 (2011): http://pn.psychiatryonline.org /content/46/7/11.1.full.

9. Mark Moran, "BPD Researcher Searches for Puzzle's Missing Piece," *Psychiatric News* 46, no. 9 (2011): http://psychiatryonline.org/newsarticle.aspx?articleid=108570.

10. Andrew W. Hoffecker, ed., *Revolutions in Worldview: Understanding the Flow of Western Thought* (Phillipsburg, NJ: P&R Publishing, 2007), xii.

A good man out of the good treasure of his heart brings forth good; and an evil man out of the evil treasure of his heart brings forth evil. For out of the abundance of the heart his mouth speaks. (Luke 6:45)

But each one is tempted when he is drawn away by his *own* desires and enticed. Then, when desire has conceived, it gives birth to sin; and sin, when it is full-grown, brings forth death. (James 1:14–15)

In Hebrews 4:12–13, God provides a biblical MRI of the heart:

For the word of God is living and active. Sharper than any double-edged sword, it penetrates even to dividing soul and spirit, joints and marrow; it judges the thoughts and attitudes of the heart. Nothing in all creation is hidden from God's sight. Everything is uncovered and laid bare before the eyes of him to whom we must give account. (NIV)

Sin is not just doing "bad" things, however:

According to the Bible, sin is . . . the breaking of a relationship, and even more, it is a rejection of God himself—a repudiation of God's rule, God's care, God's authority, and God's right to command those to whom he gave life. In short, it is the rebellion of the creature against his Creator.[11]

Although the biblical MRI shows evil spots on our hearts, that is good news because

if it comes from the heart, it is sin. If the problem is sin, there is no human remedy. No counselor, pastor, or friend

---

11. Greg Gilbert, *What Is the Gospel?* (Wheaton, IL: Crossway, 2010), 49.

can get rid of sin. But, if sin is your problem, it is the simplest thing in the world to deal with. Why? Because Jesus came for the express purpose of dealing with sin. God's Word says: "She will bring forth a Son, and you shall call His name Jesus, for He will save His people from their sin." (Matt. 1:21)[12]

So whether psychology puts the blame, or cause, of a disorder such as BPD on past abuse or on a misfiring brain, these verses show us that those things do not *cause* us to sin; instead, the cause is our own hearts filled with evil desires. That is why Proverbs 4:23 exhorts us, "Keep your heart with all diligence, for out of it spring the issues of life." As we examine the difference between BPD treatment based on psychological theories and "treatment" founded in Scripture, we will see that only God's treatment can keep our hearts with all diligence.

DSM-IV BPD SYMPTOMS ADDRESSED BY SCRIPTURE

The chart below gives a summary of the nine borderline symptoms from the *DSM-IV*[13] experienced by BPD persons and a summary of the Bible's cause and cure for those same problems. The "What God wants" section is full of Scriptures to be given for homework to BPD people by their team helpers—*experienced* and *spiritually mature* people who have a mix of the spiritual gifts of mercy, encouragement, and prophecy (speaking truth in love). The purpose of the homework is for BPD people to learn to walk in the gospel truth they are learning as their helpers incarnate truth with loving support and encouragement. Below the chart, additional biblical help is given regarding each symptom.

12. Henry Brandt and Kerry Skinner, *The Word for the Wise: Making Scripture the Heart of Your Counseling Ministry* (Nashville: Broadman & Holman, 1995), 99.
13. *Quick Reference to the Diagnostic Criteria from DSM-IV* (Washington, DC: American Psychiatric Association, 1994).

BORDERLINE PERSONALITY DISORDER

Symptom feeling/action that needs to be "put off" Eph. 4:20–24	Typical trigger/ situation	How person reacts	What person's heart wants/desires/ "deserves" (at any cost, even if destructive and possibly sinful*)	What God wants person's heart to "put on" (since he bought the person at the cost of his own life)
1. Identity disturbance: markedly and persistently unstable self-image or sense of self	I have often been victimized by childhood sexual or physical abuse in my family or by others. I may have also been physically or emotionally abandoned as a child.	I either "worship" (am addicted to) others and cling to them in an attempt to get the acceptance and love I missed in my own family, or I push them away to punish them for not giving me what I think I must have. My identity fluctuates since it is dependent on how I am treated by others at any given time.	I demand that you give me identity, worth, and value as a person. I deserve it, since I have been victimized. What God says is my identity holds no weight for me. *pride; unbelief; distrust; jealousy; complaining; anger; hopelessness; despair	My identity is in Christ: Acts 10:15 1 Cor. 6:9b–11 2 Cor. 5:17 Eph. 1:1–8 Phil. 2:1–11 2 Peter 1:3–9 1 John 3:1–2a

Feeling	Trigger	Reaction	Heart demands	What God says
2. Chronic feelings of emptiness	I don't feel that any-one cares for me or is available to me, and that provokes my feelings of being alone, disconnected, and like a bottomless pit of nothingness or neediness. I feel numb or dead, and I must desperately hang on to you so that I feel alive.	I attach myself either to people (by sex and/or clinging) or to things (other addictions [idolatries]), even if I am harmed by doing so. I feel alive only when I create enough chaos in my life to affect myself and oth-ers negatively.	I need to feel like I am alive! I may even hurt myself in order to feel alive, since "no one cares about me anyway." *faithlessness: unbe-lief; lack of self-control; violence; hopeless-ness; despair	I have been redeemed from emptiness; I have a purpose in life: John 10:10 1 Cor. 15:58 2 Cor. 5:20 Eph. 4:13; 5:18 Phil. 1:21 + "one another" Scriptures: John 13:34–35 Rom. 12:5, 10, 16; 13:8; 14:13, 19; 15:5, 7, 14 1 Cor. 12:25 Gal. 5:15, 26; 6:2 Eph. 4:25, 32; 5:21 Col. 3:9, 13 1 Thess. 4:18 Titus 3:3 Heb. 10:24 James 5:9, 16 1 Peter 4:9; 5:5 1 John 3:11, 23; 4:7, 11-12

| 3. Frantic efforts to avoid real or imagined abandonment | If the person I desire does not respond immediately to my demands (whatever they are), I feel abandoned. I feel rejected, like you are paying more attention to someone else than me. | I rage at the person I think abandons me and get very depressed, even suicidal, and I will generally act out in destructive ways. I must punish either you for abandonment or myself because I feel needy (and that is unacceptable to me). | I desire never to feel abandoned and always to feel connected! But even if you try to connect with me and show me that you will not abandon me, I will still test you to see if you mean it. You must love me incessantly and unconditionally for me to feel secure (although you can never do enough for me for that to happen). Again, God's promises of nonabandonment hold no weight in my life.

*faithlessness; jealousy; factiousness; lack of self-control; anger; malice; rage; ingratitude; bitterness; hopelessness | God will never abandon me; he is my Savior, not others; I need not act out when I feel abandoned; he will provide others to care for me:
Pss. 23; 27:10; 46:1–2; 68:5–6, 18
Isa. 43:1; 49:15; 66:13
Ezek. 34:2, 4–5
John 14:18
Rom. 8:31–39; 15:4
Eph. 4:26, 30
Heb. 6:19
James 1:19–20
1 Peter 5:2–3 |

Feeling	Trigger	Reaction	Heart demands	What God says
4. Affective instability due to a marked reactivity of mood (e.g., intense episodic dysphoria, irritability, or anxiety usually lasting a few hours and only rarely more than a few days)	Life isn't working the way I want it to, so I get irritable and anxious because I do not know how to fix it. I have no choice but to feel intensely anxious or irritable if you do not give me what I think I need to feel better. But even when I get what I want, the good feelings don't last.	I can't figure out what's going on; I feel out of control and up and down. I am full of anxiety and irritability. You need to fix me so that I don't feel so bad.	I don't want to have any bad feelings—although I feel empty if there isn't chaos in my life. *anxiety; lack of hope and self-control; envy; impatience	God supplies me with peace that passes understanding: Pss. 34:14; 71:4–5; 119:165 Prov. 14:30 Isa. 26:3 John 14:27; 16:33 Rom. 5:1; 15:13 Eph. 2:14 Phil. 4:6–7 Col. 1:20; 3:15 2 Thess. 3:16 1 Peter 3:11 1 John 1:9

| 5. A pattern of unstable and intense interpersonal relationships characterized by alternating between extremes of idealization and devaluation | When you please me, I will idolize you as "all good." When you displease me, I will devalue you as "all bad." And I do the same thing to myself: I'm either "all good" or "all bad," depending on how I perform and what you think of me [this is called "splitting"]. | I understand life only in black and white. I have no gray areas. I either love you or hate you—or both: "I hate you; don't leave me"* | I want to feel secure in relationships, but that happens only if you please me or are pleased with me. But even if I think you are pleased with me, I will test you in various ways (usually destructive) to see if you really care about me.

*selfishness; bitter envy; lack of self-control; impatience; evil thoughts; spiteful-ness; complaining; gossip; contentious-ness; slandering | Others *will* disappoint me; no one but God is perfect and totally trustworthy:
Pss. 31:1; 56:3–4, 11; 146:3–4
Prov. 29:25
Isa. 44:9–28
Matt. 10:26, 28
James 4:1–10 |

* Jerold J. Kreisman and Hal Straus, I *Hate You—Don't Leave Me* (Los Angeles: Body Press, 1989).

Feeling	Trigger	Reaction	Heart demands	What God says
6. Inappropriate intense anger or difficulty controlling anger (e.g., frequent displays of temper, constant anger, recurrent physical fights)	You hurt me, and I use my intense anger (temper tantrum) to punish and control you so that I will get my way! Hateful resentment is a way of life for me.	When you displease me, I will likely rage at you and may even get into a physical fight with you. If I don't hit you, I may hit myself. You must understand that it is your fault, not mine; I cannot control my rage.	I want you to give me what I want so that I don't feel bad. It doesn't matter how you feel. I never think about how my behavior affects anyone else, only how yours affects me. *selfishness; anger, resentment; violence; rage; lack of self-control; disputing; bitter envy; quarrelsomeness	My anger does not bring about God's righteousness: Gal. 5:19–21 Eph. 4:29–32 James 1:19–20; 3:13–18

Symptom			I want you to tell me	Scripture
7. Transient, stress-related paranoid ideation or severe dissociative symptoms	I may be incredibly fearful if you don't do what you said you would (even if you don't think you said it). I should be kept from all harm.	The only way I think I can deal with my feelings of abandonment is to dissociate (be out of touch with reality). Or I may also feel paranoid and suspicious of your motives and withdraw from you in fear.	I want you to tell me that what I think and feel is real, although I will doubt what you say. I want you to know that I am afraid of you and don't trust you. *lack of trust; suspicion; lack of love; faithlessness; fearfulness; evil thoughts; lack of self-control	God is sovereign: Gen. 18:13–14; 45:8; 50:20 2 Chron. 20:6–9 Job 3:25; 12:7–25 Pss. 23; 139 Prov. 1:7; 3:25–26; 16:23; 29:25 Jer. 29:11 Dan. 3:17; 4:24–37; 5:18–31 John 3:3–8 Acts 2:23; 4:28; 17:24–28 Eph. 1:11; 2:10 1 John 4:18
8. Impulsivity in at least two areas that are potentially self-damaging	I need you to give me what I want *now* because I am hurting and you should give me what I want/need when I want it.	When I decide to do something, I go for it then and there. I want instant gratification; I don't consider that there may be adverse consequences.	No one is going to change my mind: I want what I want! I do not want you to tell me that what I want or how I act is childish, self-destructive, or unrealistic. *impatience; selfish ambition; greed; lust; ingratitude; rebelliousness	God desires me to be mature rather than childish: Pss. 130:5; 131 Prov. 22:15 Rom. 6:11–18 1 Cor. 13:11; 14:20 James 1:3–8 1 Peter 1:13–14

Feeling	Trigger	Reaction	Heart demands	What God says
9. Recurrent suicidal behavior, gestures, or threats, or self-mutilating behavior	When I feel betrayed by you, my feelings are too intense to handle. I can't live with them, so I think I must do something to make them go away now.	The stress, hurt, or anger is too painful for me to handle. I can make those feelings go away (temporarily) through self-destructive behaviors. If those don't work, then I'll threaten to or attempt suicide; there is no other option for me.	I do not want to feel any pain. I do not know how to comfort myself other than punishing myself to numb the pain or to feel the adrenaline rush when being self-destructive. *fearfulness; lack of trust; selfishness; lack of love; lack of self-control; rebelliousness; disobedience; violence	I belong to the Lord, and he both promises and provides a way of escape: Ex. 20:3 1 Cor. 6:19–20; 7:23; 10:13 2 Cor. 10:3–5 Heb. 4:15–16

Additional Scriptures of Hope

Pss. 39:7; 130:5–8; 146:5–7; Lam. 3:21–27; Rom. 5:2–5; 15:13; Col. 1:19–27; 1 Thess. 5:8; 2 Thess. 2:16–17; 1 Tim. 1:1; Titus 1:2; 2:13; 3:7; Heb. 3:6; 6:18–19; 11:1; 1 Peter 1:3, 21; 3:15; 1 John 3:3

Each of the nine BPD symptoms is addressed below in more detail; heart Scriptures to "put on" in place of each symptom or behavior that needs to be "put off" (Eph. 4:20–24) are found in the chart above. The symptoms below have been divided into four clusters: Disturbed Identity; Disturbed Mood; Disturbed Perception; and Disturbed Behavior.[14]

DISTURBED IDENTITY

1. Identity disturbance: markedly and persistently unstable self-image or sense of self.

Biblical Goal: "Learn to live in my identity in Christ."

As helpers begin to establish relationships with BPD persons (no easy feat, since BPD persons have difficulty trusting others), the helpers need to follow Paul's example to be "gentle [with them], just as a nursing mother cherishes her own children," and to exhort and comfort them, "as a father does his own children" (1 Thess. 2:7, 11).

(Note: To find out whether helpers really care for them, BPD persons will consistently "test" them with various destructive behaviors. Other members of the team should *always* be brought in when this happens so that the helper being "tested" isn't provoked into doing something unwise.)

Often BPD persons have been victimized in horrendous ways, and their identity is that of a victim. Even though they

14. Richard A. Moskovitz, *Lost in the Mirror: An Inside Look at Borderline Personality Disorder* (Dallas: Taylor, 1996), 33.

are Christians, they have a difficult time trusting that either helpers or God loves them and that they actually *are* who God says they are. In their minds, they are who they *feel* like they are at any given moment. So they must be assisted to learn that they do not have the right to call *anything (including themselves) unclean that God has made clean* (Acts 10:15) and that their identity is no longer what it was before they came to know Christ.

David Needham states that, unlike any other birth, the new birth enjoys the benefit that the umbilical cord between us and God is "never severed."[15] God's plan is for us always to stay attached to him for life and sustenance. BPD persons (and all the rest of us, at one time or another) get into trouble when they (functionally) unhook their umbilical cord and try to attach it to someone or something else. If that someone else tries to give the BPD person life (so to speak), he or she will be drained because only God can provide all that we need (2 Peter 1:3–10).

Another big problem in getting BPD persons to walk in their identity in Christ is that they don't *feel* as though they belong to Christ. According to Bill Gillham, "the devil's definition of a hypocrite is 'anyone who acts contrary to how he *feels*.'"[16] That is, feelings are considered truth, so if one acts differently from how he or she *feels*, that person is a hypocrite. But Gillham reminds us that rather than those who act differently from how they *feel*, hypocrites are defined as those who act differently from *who they are* (1 John 3:1), no matter what they have experienced in the past. For example:

---

15. David Needham, *Birthright: Christian, Do You Know Who You Are?* (Sisters, OR: Multnomah, 1999), 140.

16. Bill Gillham, *Lifetime Guarantee: Making Your Christian Life Work and What to Do When It Doesn't* (Brentwood, TN: Wolgemuth & Hyatt, 1987), 117.

The pain of child abuse extends far beyond physical or sexual damage; *betrayal of trust* sends shocking waves of anguish, fear, anger, rage, and temptations to react throughout the victim's life. . . . Yet what is even more devastating than the abuse itself is the way some have allowed it to define their lives: nursing bitterness; committing to revenge; desperately searching—even demanding!—affirmation against deep-seated, stubborn insecurities; believing that "I must have deserved this," carrying guilt that belongs to the abuser alone; believing that "*victim* is who I am at the core." . . . [But] we need to be able to talk about it, grieve it, and find grace and mercy in our time of need.[17]

2. Chronic feelings of emptiness.

Biblical Goal: "I have been redeemed from emptiness: I have a new purpose in life."

The emptiness that BPD persons feel is due to feeling disconnected from others and alone in the universe. As Christians, however, BPD persons have been redeemed from empty lives and have a new purpose in life: bringing glory to God. Feelings of emptiness bring on addictions of all kinds because they think they need someone or something to help them either fill up or numb their emptiness. One young woman diagnosed with BPD commented to me, "I want to crawl into [my] boyfriend's skin so I can feel like a real person."

But just as "this manna" (Num. 11:5) or even "the bread of life" (John 6:32–35) did not suffice for the Israelites, God's gifts do not feel like enough for BPD persons.[18] Why? Because "it is always tempting to find fullness in something other than Christ. Often I opt for peace and comfort rather than Jesus. . . . [But] Paul says that we have been given fullness in

17. Wilkerson, *Redemption*, 22–23.
18. Timothy S. Lane and Paul David Tripp, *How People Change* (Winston-Salem, NC: Punch, 2006), 125.

[him]. If I act on this truth, nothing can empty me of what is already mine."[19]

3. Frantic efforts to avoid real or imagined abandonment.

Biblical Goal: "I must learn to trust that God will never abandon me even though humans will. Therefore, I do not have to act out when I feel abandoned."

No one likes to be rejected or abandoned. For those labeled with BPD, however, it feels like the end of the world, an absolutely catastrophic occurrence. BPD persons avoid abandonment at all costs as they cling to or withdraw from the person perceived as causing the abandonment. The one who (apparently) abandons them must be "punished," so they react with rage or depression, or fluctuate between the two.

BPD persons can learn that Christ will never abandon them. It is also important for helpers to become examples of nonabandonment themselves as they make sure (to the best of their human abilities) that they keep their word to BPD persons. Know, however, that helpers *will* disappoint BPD persons because helpers are human and because BPD persons have totally unrealistic expectations and demands. Again, that is why it is beneficial to deal with a BPD person as a team.

BPD persons need to learn that God gives them the power to repent of the rage or despair they feel rather than being ruled by either, since God reassures them that they will never be abandoned. They must also learn that God's forgiveness, presence, and comfort are available *always*.

God calls shepherds to take care of all his sheep, and he is very serious about the kind of care those shepherds provide. BPD persons are quick to blame others for their problems, so they might use the following verses as ammunition to

19. Paul David Tripp, *Lost in the Middle: MidLife and the Grace of God* (Wapwallopen, PA: Shepherd Press, 2004), 32–33.

blame their shepherds for not caring for them "the way they should!" Nevertheless, it is helpful for them to know that God wants shepherds to serve as "overseers, not by compulsion but willingly, not for dishonest gain but eagerly; nor as being lords over those entrusted to [them], but being examples to the flock" (1 Peter 5:2–3). Ezekiel 34 outlines the severe consequences that God gives to shepherds who abandon their flocks!

Additionally, shepherds should not abandon their flocks to the world's care or its wisdom; in fact, "the church is in trouble when its designated experts in the cure of souls are mental health professionals who owe their legitimacy to the state" because God has given "the church [the] responsibility for these people's lives."[20]

DISTURBED MOOD

4. Affective instability due to a marked reactivity of mood (e.g., intense episodic dysphoria [unpleasant mood], irritability, or anxiety usually lasting a few hours and only rarely more than a few days).

Biblical Goal: "I do not have to live in chaos; I can experience peace that passes understanding."

Lack of peace and feeling irritable, anxious, and fearful generally happen when BPD persons' feelings (regardless of why) are not pleasing to them. Chaos and panic follow quickly as they desperately pursue someone to make them feel better.

Although we generally think of peace as an absence of conflicting or painful feelings, listen to this profound definition: "Biblically speaking, peace is not the absence of conflict, but

20. David Powlison, "Cure of Souls (and the Modern Psychotherapies)," *Journal of Biblical Counseling* 25, no. 2 (2007): 30.

the absence of sin."[21] You get the idea: when we confess and are forgiven of our sin, we experience peace with God—which does not necessarily mean that we instantly feel good. For an example, think of Jesus in Gethsemane (Matt. 26:39).

Paul prays in Philippians 4:9, "Whatever you have learned or received or heard from me, or seen in me—put it into practice. And the God of peace will be with you" (NIV). We don't just pray a prayer or quote a verse and, *abracadabra*, we feel peace. The miracle of experiencing "peace . . . which transcends all understanding" (4:7 NIV) happens as we *practice* God's Word (in spite of our feelings) as he gives us the grace to obey.

5. A pattern of unstable and intense interpersonal relationships characterized by alternating between extremes of idealization and devaluation.

Biblical Goal: "I know that others will disappoint me because no one but God is perfect and trustworthy."

Alternating between idealization and devaluation is called *splitting*. Those labeled with BPD have a difficult time seeing gray areas. Everything and everyone is seen as black ("all bad") or white ("all good"). This means that either the person or the helper can be perceived as wonderful (idealized) one minute and trash (devalued) the next! When this happens, it makes it difficult to continue caring about the person who just trashed you when you were only trying to help. But remember that helpers must not base their responses on feelings, either.

Another helpful concept to know about that contributes to BPD persons' "intense interpersonal relationships" is called *projective identification*. Most people know what *projection* is:

21. Winston Smith, "Getting the Big Picture of Relationships," *Journal of Biblical Counseling* 22, no. 3 (2004): 12.

attributing one's unacceptable emotion or thought to someone else. In projective identification, however, one person "projects" his or her emotions and the other "identifies" with them as his or her own. In other words, when BPD persons project (unknowingly) their own unacceptable feelings or impulses onto their helpers (or family members or others), the helpers actually feel and perceive those (usually intense/destructive) feelings as their own (rather than the BPD persons') and feel the urgency to act on those feelings to help the BPD persons.

This pattern of behavior may have begun in the BPD persons' families of origin when parents' or others' strong feelings were projected onto them. All children feel the need to make their parents "okay" because that is where their security lies. And helpers who grow up in families where they also felt "on guard" all the time will be more susceptible to this experience. So take note: If a helper feels an intense, immediate need to take care of the BPD person or experiences anger that seems much "too big" for the situation, the helper may be experiencing projective identification.

Again, the team is helpful here to keep the other member grounded in reality and also because the BPD person "splits" helpers with comments such as: "You're the only one who ever understood me. I'll tell you things that I wouldn't tell _____." The helper feels special, thinking he or she has gained the BPD person's trust, but the helper is actually being split from the team by keeping confidences that he or she should not keep.

BPD persons should be taught that others in their lives are not God but are sinners who will never respond perfectly to their desires. Like all the rest of us, BPD persons must learn to make wise choices about those with whom they are in relationships. God gives us many principles in his Word so that we can learn when someone is there to help or hurt us. BPD persons must learn to pay attention to "red flags" by observing a person's lifestyle to see whether the person more consistently lives in the Spirit or in the flesh. Most importantly, BPD persons need to learn that if they are looking to others to make them feel good about themselves, then others become their gods. But those "gods" cannot produce peaceful hearts.

6. Inappropriate intense anger or difficulty controlling anger (e.g., frequent displays of temper, constant anger, recurrent physical fights).

Biblical Goal: "My anger does not bring about God's righteousness, nor do I have the right to take vengeance."

To most BPD persons, anger feels like an uncontrollable knee-jerk reaction that they can't help. They sound very much like St. Augustine in his description of his own rage. As an infant, Augustine

> "was indignant with my elders for not submitting to me, with those owing me no service, for not serving me, and avenged myself on them by tears. . . .
>
> "Or bitterly to resent that . . . the very authors of my birth did not serve me . . . [and even though] wiser than me, did not obey the nod of my good pleasure. . . .
>
> "The weakness then of an infant's limbs, not its will, is its innocence." What makes us call an infant "innocent?" It is his inability to rise up and punch the person who doesn't feed him on demand, not his innocent heart. An infant's heart would throw a right hook if his arms were strong enough. . . . Why make such a big thing over all this? . . . [Because] childhood "innocence" soon yields to riper adolescent and adult selfishness. When a child's formerly "innocent" limbs become as developed as his always-demanding heart, be ready for fully developed displays of rage![22]

22. Robert D. Jones, *Uprooting Anger: Biblical Help for a Common Problem* (Phillipsburg, NJ: P&R Publishing, 2005), 53–54.

Helpers who hear a BPD person's sad and often tragic story (which must always be heard compassionately) may consider the BPD person innocent. Although there may be extenuating circumstances, however, helpers must remember that we cannot blame others for our own sinful responses and that "even a child is known by his deeds, whether what he does is pure and right" (Prov. 20:11).

John MacArthur comments on rage in Galatians 5:19–21: " 'Hatred' results in 'contentions' (strife); 'jealousies' (hateful resentment) result in 'outbursts of wrath' (sudden unrestrained expressions of hostility). 'Envy, murder, drunkenness, orgies, and the like' represent animosity between individuals and groups."[23] All these descriptions of anger and rage are part of the BPD person's lifestyle. But no matter the provocation, God does not give any Christian the right to take revenge (or throw a temper tantrum) because vengeance belongs only to him. We know that anger yields more anger.

DISTURBED PERCEPTION

7. Transient, stress-related paranoid ideation or severe dissociative symptoms.

Biblical Goal: "God is sovereign over my life, so I can trust him to take care of me."

Since those with BPD can have dissociative symptoms (feelings of unreality or split consciousness), one may be inclined to wonder whether they have dissociative identity disorder (DID, previously called MPD/multiple personality disorder). The difference is that the periods of dissociation associated with BPD are brief rather than ongoing.

23. John MacArthur, ed., *The MacArthur Study Bible* (Nashville: Thomas Nelson, 1997), 1798.

BPD persons are attuned to the slightest rejection, so it is easy for them to feel paranoid and "'make mountains out of molehills,' [be] argumentative, and . . . always [be] ready to counterattack at the slightest hint of potential threat or criticism."[24] Some synonyms for *paranoia* are *suspicion, fear, mistrust, unreasonableness,* and *obsession.* People who suffer from it are inclined to think Job's thoughts after him: "for the thing I greatly feared has come upon me" (Job 3:25). They are self-protective and do not trust that the plans God has for them are good and not evil (Jer. 29:11).

DISTURBED BEHAVIOR

8. Impulsivity in at least two areas that are potentially self-damaging.

Biblical Goal: "I need to mature in Christ and experience self-control as a fruit of the Spirit."

Impulsivity is the hallmark of a child or immature person who has not learned self-control. Even though BPD persons *feel* like children much of the time, they can learn that they are not and can learn to act like adults regardless of their feelings. This doesn't mean that their helpers do not empathize with their strong feelings of impulsivity; it means that they help BPD persons learn to respond to truth rather than their feelings when those disagree with Scripture.

When we feel compelled to obey our feelings, they become our gods. But God can transform our hearts as we look to him:

When you allow Jesus to come into your body as your Savior, not only are you cleansed from your sin, but you

24. Raymond J. Corsini and Alan J. Auerbach, *Concise Encyclopedia of Psychology* (New York: John Wiley & Sons, Inc., 1998), 620.

also have access to the Spirit of God. Here is an invisible, unexplainable presence that produces visible, measurable changes in the way your body works. Your body is transformed. Phillip Keller describes this miracle: "deceivers become honest; the vile become noble; the vicious become gentle; the selfish become selfless; the hard-hearted become affectionate; the weak become strong. . . . Apart from the Spirit of God in control, human beings' ill will, hatred, bitterness, envy, old grudges, jealousy and other heinous attitudes can be masked with a casual shrug or forced half smile."

Nothing in this world can cause a person to change so radically. No longer do circumstances or people determine the condition under your skin. You can now respond to the troublesome people in your life with unconditional love, joy, peace, long-suffering, kindness, goodness, faithfulness, gentleness, and self-control. By yielding to the Spirit of God, an infinite, endless supply flows through you. There is enough for a minor irritation or a major tragedy.[25]

So BPD persons can change radically as they choose to believe that the label *borderline* does not define them, but *child of God* does, because they are no longer his enemies:

Ashamed of your many years at the Dragon's side, you stood off to the side alone [feeling abandoned], gazing at the ground until Jesus came to you. Taking your chin in his hand, Jesus lifted your face, looked you in the eye, and told you that your sins were forgiven, your Enemy conquered, and your life liberated from captivity, and that God is now your Father, new life is your gift, and heaven is your home. As tears streamed down your face, Jesus asked you always to remember to see yourself as he does, not in light of what you have done or what has been done

25. Brandt and Skinner, *The Word for the Wise*, 176.

to you, but rather solely by what he has done for you as your victorious Warrior King.[26]

9. Recurrent suicidal behavior, gestures, or threats, or self-mutilating behavior.

Biblical Goal: "I belong to the Lord, and he will provide a way of escape for me."

Often BPD persons believe that threatening (or attempting) suicide is the only possible escape from their pain. One BPD woman I was seeing attempted suicide by overdosing when I did not call her right back one night even though another therapist was the one on call. I had told her that I would be at the hospital that night because my grandchild was being born. This BPD woman was in ICU for over a week before she regained consciousness. The helper may never know for sure if the person is "just" making a threat, but a threat should never be ignored. It is a myth that if someone threatens suicide, he or she will not carry it out. The helper should always ask whether the person has a plan for suicide. If he or she replies "yes," the threat is more serious. The helper must always call 911 if in doubt about the person's safety.

Self-mutilating behavior, such as cutting, is another way for BPD persons to feel alive or to escape from pain (those who do this say that cutting "feels good"). For those who cut, it "is [often] the only release [they] know; so [they] cut themselves deeper and deeper, trying to bleed out all that pain."[27]

As Edward Welch states, "self-abusers typically want to live; they just don't know how to live with turbulent emotions."[28] He encourages those who self-injure to

26. Mark Driscoll and Gerry Breshears, *Death by Love: Letters from the Cross* (Wheaton, IL: Crossway, 2010), 46.

27. Wilkerson, *Redemption*, 2.

28. Edward T. Welch, "Self-Injury: When Pain Feels Good," *Journal of Biblical Counseling* 22, no. 2 (2004): 32.

slow down and consider what is happening. The self-injury cycle has its reasons, but it quickly becomes automatic. Your emotions tell you what to do and you robotically respond. Lies become a way of life that distances you from people who love you and could help you. Yes, slowing down can seem dangerous when your inner screams are getting louder and you feel that your only escape may soon be blocked. But there is another way. It is a path of wisdom, and wise people begin it by considering their ways.[29]

Of course, when someone is caught in this cycle, it is difficult to stop it. But biblical wisdom is available to BPD persons as they allow others who love them to be with them and teach them these truths:

> You don't injure yourself for the good of others. Instead, it is about you and how you make your own life work. . . . If you keep moving back into self-injury, notice how your behavior is more intentional than it seems. You are doing what you want to do. If you are not learning from past self-abuse, you don't want to change. For example, are you putting barriers between yourself and your self-abuse strategies?[30]

"Barriers" are those who remind self-abusers that their own "sin-stained blood could never atone, could never soothe [their] guilty conscience, could never satisfy the wrath of a holy God, could never make a pure plea for God's rescue."[31] After all, God doesn't "barely save" us by "technically sparing [us] from hell in the end but practically leaving [us] hopeless in the meantime."[32]

And "barriers" are those who remind self-abusers that they "have a great High Priest who [was abused in their place and

29. Ibid.
30. Ibid., 35, 40.
31. Wilkerson, *Redemption*, 72.
32. Ibid., 155.

who] . . . sympathize[s] with [their] weaknesses" so that they "may obtain mercy and find grace to help in time of need" (Heb. 4:14–16).

PSYCHOLOGICAL TREATMENTS

Various treatments are used for BPD, since treatment is based on the psychological theory to which each counselor adheres. Whichever theory a counselor follows, however, research literature reveals that the prognosis for the person with BPD is very poor and generally requires long-term treatment (eight to ten years):

> Treatment for this disorder is long term in nature since the symptoms have been present for an extended time and interfere with many aspects of the person's life. Insight oriented therapy can be helpful but research is showing an increased support for a cognitive-behavioral approach. In other words, the individual's thoughts and actions are monitored both by the self and therapist and specific behaviors are counted and a plan is made to gradually reduce those thoughts and behaviors that are seen as negative. A combined approach may be best, but either way requires intensive time and effort. . . . Long term treatment is almost always required.[33]

But newer researchers state that "the first trial-and-error years of treating borderline patients [have] seen a rapid expansion of knowledge about the genetic and neurobiological correlates of BPD."[34] Additionally, the knowledge gained from the perspective of neuroscience confirms that BPD persons can be

33. AllPsych.com, "Borderline Personality Disorder" (2011), available at http://allpsych.com/disorders/personality/borderline.html.
34. Mark Moran, "Long Journey Led to Advances in Understanding, Treating BPD," *Psychiatric News* 46, no. 6 (2011): http://psychiatryonline.org/newsarticle.aspx?articleid=108369.

helped to use their prefrontal cortex to think through and process their highly emotional thoughts and behaviors (possibly from an overactive amygdala). For this reason, one psychologist claims that all psychotherapies are helpful, since they "involve talking directly to the brain."[35]

Some forms of psychotherapy that have proved effective for BPD symptoms are "dialectical behavior therapy; mentalization-based therapy, transference-focused therapy, schema-focused therapy, supportive psychotherapy, systems training for emotional predictability and problem solving (STEPPS), and general psychiatric management with dynamically oriented therapy."[36]

According to empirical research, all these treatments are helpful. Marsha Linehan, PhD, recently developed a therapy that she calls dialectical behavior therapy (DET). Dr. Linehan was hospitalized at a young age for problems that she now believes should have been diagnosed as BPD. From her own experience and research, she believes "real change [is] possible [for BPD patients]. The emerging discipline of behaviorism taught that people could learn new behaviors and that acting differently can in time alter underlying emotions."[37] Dr. Linehan calls behaviorism "emerging," but it was "launched by J. B. Watson in 1913, [after having] already begun in the work of [earlier] psychologists."[38]

While some hail DET as a great help for BPD, others say that it is definitely not a miracle cure.[39] DET and most of the other treatments do show some success in that "a substantial majority of patients with BPD experience remission of symptoms and that

35. Moran, "Gabbard Weds Neurobiology Psychodynamics in BPD Treatment."

36. Moran, "Long Journey Led to Advances in Understanding, Treating BPD."

37. Tara Parker-Pope, "Coming Out with Mental Illness" (2011), available at http://well.blogs.nytimes.com/2011/06/23/coming-out-with-mental-illness/?ref=health.

38. Corsini and Auerbach, *Concise Encyclopedia of Psychology*, 87.

39. Randi Kreger, "Stop Walking on Eggshells: When Someone in Your Life Has Borderline or Narcissistic Personality Disorder" (2011), available at http://www.psychologytoday.com/blog/stop-walking-eggshells.

their remission tends to be stable over time . . . but crucially, the study also found that only half of patients achieve good social and vocational functioning [and] may remain unable to maintain close long-term relationships or a job."[40]

Although these psychotherapies help with BPD symptoms, they do not provide a cure. Many people, however, think brain research will show that medication provides a cure. While it is true that medication can "relieve some significantly debilitating symptoms [it is] not expected to alter longstanding personality characteristics or behavior."[41] Another psychiatrist simply states, "There is no drug for BPD. Drugs may sometimes be helpful for treating specific symptoms of BPD or acute illness that may occur during the course of BPD."[42] So neither psychotherapies nor medication is a cure for BPD, and since there are many side effects from psychotropic medication, one should consider both the risk and the benefit of using medication for symptom relief.

Exercise, as well as nutrition (both good diet and health supplements), has proved to be beneficial for depression, anxiety, and mood swings. Since God tells us that our bodies are his temple and we are responsible to glorify him with them (1 Cor. 6:19–20; 10:31), it would be wise to pursue research in these less dangerous areas of help. (See nutrition/medication resources at end of booklet.)

TIPS FOR BIBLICAL HELPERS

A team of three or four biblical helpers, rather than an individual helper, is the most effective way to work with BPD persons. This is true for the following reasons:

40. Mark Moran, "BPD Researcher Searches for Puzzle's Missing Piece."
41. Kreisman Straus, *I Hate You—Don't Leave Me*, 139.
42. Moskovitz, *Lost in the Mirror*, 111.

1. Although they don't mean to be, BPD persons are very draining. For that reason, the team of helpers can encourage and pray for one another as they persevere in love and grace with BPD persons.

2. BPD persons try to "split" their helpers (see #5 in chart and #5 under the "Disturbed Mood" section above), so the team *must* commit never to keep anything confidential between any one of them and a BPD person. The best situation is for more than one on the team to always be in interaction with the BPD person at any given time (i.e., no one on the team should ever make a decision regarding the person without consulting with another team member).

3. Helpers will get angry as they feel "used" by the (usually ungrateful) BPD person, yet they are still called to be examples of the fruit of the Spirit. As their own hearts are tested, tried, and provoked, they will need God's grace to walk in the Spirit and to model that walk to those to whom they wish to minister:

> What shall we say then? Shall we continue in sin that grace may abound? Certainly not! How shall we who died to sin live any longer in it? . . . Therefore do not let sin reign in your mortal body, that you should obey it in its lusts. And do not present your members as instruments of unrighteousness to sin, but present yourselves to God as being alive from the dead, and your members as instruments of righteousness to God. For sin shall not have dominion over you, *for you are not under law but under grace.* (Rom. 6:1–2, 12–14)

4. All helpers must teach BPD persons that Scripture is not law ("just do it"—that is, "what God wants from them is morality") but that it is the "gloriously liberating and

life-changing truths of the gospel."[43] Then they will begin to experience

> what happens when we live God's way[.] He brings gifts into our lives, much the same way that fruit appears in an orchard—things like affection for others, exuberance about life, serenity. We develop a willingness to stick with things, a sense of compassion in the heart, and a conviction that a basic holiness permeates things and people. We find ourselves involved in loyal commitments, not needing to force our way in life, able to marshal and direct our energies wisely. Legalism is helpless in bringing this about; it only gets in the way. Among those who belong to Christ, everything connected with getting our own way and mindlessly responding to what everyone else calls necessities is killed off for good—crucified. Since this is the kind of life we have chosen, the life of the Spirit, let us make sure that we do not just hold it as an idea in our heads or a sentiment in our hearts, but work out its implications in every detail of our lives. That means we will not compare ourselves with each other as if one of us were better and another worse. (Gal. 5:22–26 *The Message*)

5. Helpers should be aware that anyone who has previously worked with this disorder will erroneously believe that "the problems are too deep for biblical counseling."[44] But helpers must have confidence that they have "been redeemed by Jesus, [and] bear a message of hope that is unmatched by any therapy, medication, or support group the world has to offer."[45]

43. Elyse M. Fitzpatrick and Jessica Thompson, *Give Them Grace: Dazzling Your Kids with the Love of Jesus* (Wheaton, IL: Crossway, 2011), 19.

44. Edward T. Welch, "Is Biblical-Nouthetic Counseling Legalistic? Reexamination of a Biblical Theme," *Journal of Pastoral Practice* 11, no. 1 (1992): 6.

45. Wilkerson, *Redemption*, 173.

6. Nearly all BPD persons are very smart and, whether high- or low-functioning, have the ability to do homework. Using the Scriptures listed above for each symptom, for example, have them write out the referenced Scripture, using their own names to personalize it, even memorizing those parts with which they particularly identify (Ps. 119:11). Also see the appendix for a sample chart illustrating a helpful way for BPD persons to organize their feelings and Scripture. They will find it a quick reference when feeling overwhelmed. Helpers should never forget that they cannot change another; it is *only through prayer, the grace of God, and the power of the Holy Spirit that heart change occurs.*

Scriptural Encouragement for Helpers

Isa. 55:13; Ezek. 34; Acts 20:24–37; Rom. 5:1–4; 15:1–6, 13; 1 Cor. 1; 2; 13; 2 Cor. 1:3–14; 3:12; Gal. 1:3–12; 3:1–13; 5:11; Col. 1; 1 Thess. 2:2–10; 2:19; Titus 2:1–3:8; James 1:5; 2:17–18; 1 Peter 3:8–17

CONCLUSION

Hope happens as a person "surrender[s] every competing hope. For the Israelites, it was the call to abandon the worship of any other god and entrust their lives to the one true God."[46] For those diagnosed with BPD, as well as their helpers, it means surrendering the competing hope of life through psychological theories/techniques or various addictions (biblically, "idolatries") for the hope found in Christ.

The world's competing hopes are counterfeit because they are based on the external hopes of therapy, circumstances, behavior, thinking, self-concept, or even thinking that "just trust Jesus

46. Ibid., 154.

more" will bring heart change.[47] Consider the advice given in the article "Bewildered by the Borderline Personality" as an example of how to help a female BPD church member causing havoc in the congregation: "Churches and their leaders can help these persons function at a higher level, manage their emotional turmoil, and disrupt the congregation less."[48]

The suggested techniques in that case were helpful: set firm limits; try not to encourage an overly personalized relationship; try not to withdraw and terminate the pastoral relationship when frustrated or fatigued. Of note, the church's consistent love for the BPD person did help her to better understand God's love as well as help the church to "carry out the scriptural injunction to love those who are difficult to love . . . [even as they learned] more about their own anger and childish qualities."[49] But notice that the church's goal for the woman was focused on helping her to "function higher . . . manage better . . . disrupt less," rather than on the biblical hope of becoming like Christ.

True hope is possible, however, "if indeed [we] continue in the faith, grounded and steadfast, and are not moved away from the *hope of the gospel* . . . [or] deceive[d] . . . with persuasive words" (Col. 1:23; 2:4). Neither biblical helpers nor those labeled with BPD should be deceived by the "many alternative theories of change that lead . . . away from Christ and His grace"[50] and bring no hope. Instead, it is

> God himself, the God of peace, [who will] sanctify you through and through. May your whole spirit, soul and body be kept blameless at the coming of our Lord Jesus Christ. The one who calls you is faithful and he will do it. (1 Thess. 5:23–24 NIV)

47. Lane and Tripp, *How People Change*, 29.

48. Enos Martin and E. A. Vastyan, "Bewildered by the Borderline Personality," *Leadership* (Fall 1989): 45.

49. Ibid., 48.

50. Lane and Tripp, *How People Change*, 36.

[So even if you struggle with being diagnosed with BPD,] if you are Christ's child, there is hope for you! It is not based on who you are or what you know. Your hope is Jesus! He lives in you and, because of that, you have a reason to celebrate each new day. You no longer live, but Christ lives in you![51]

I know that hope for change is possible because God promises it. I also know, because of my own experience with BPD persons who have hit, kicked, thrown food at, spit on, threatened (gun and knife), and choked me (among other things!), that change happened for those who learned to walk in the Spirit and rest in God's peace. And although helpers may not act out those same behaviors, *all* Christians struggle not to cross the same "borderline," the one between the flesh and the Spirit!

This means that all Christians, BPD or not, have the same heart struggle to live by faith. To do that, we must "lay hold of the hope set before us [that] we have as an anchor of the soul, both sure and steadfast" (Heb. 6:18–19), remembering that "whatever things were written before were written for our learning, that we through the patience and comfort of the Scriptures might . . . abound in hope by the power of the Holy Spirit" (Rom. 15:4, 13).

51. Ibid., 19.

APPENDIX

Sample Homework: My Feelings versus God's Word*

Feeling	Trigger	What demands, false beliefs, self-righteous feelings fuel my heart	What I must put off and put on	What God says
Sad	Anniversary of my mother's death.	I wasn't the kind of daughter I would have liked to have. My mom didn't really know me, and I didn't know her. This makes me sad. I feel guilty that I didn't make the effort to get to know her. Memories of the lonely trip to California for her funeral still make me sad after fourteen years. Everyone was happy to be going home for Christmas, but I was going home for a funeral.	I need to put off self-condemnation and put on God's forgiveness and the hope of reconciliation in heaven.	"Can I bring him back again? I shall go to him, but he shall not return to me" (2 Sam. 12:23). "All the prophets testify about him that everyone who believes in him receives forgiveness of sins through his name" (Acts 10:43 NIV). "There is therefore now no condemnation to those who are in Christ Jesus" (Rom. 8:1). "We know that the one who raised the Lord Jesus from the dead will also raise us with Jesus and present us with you in his presence" (2 Cor. 4:14 NIV).

* Used by permission of Jane Pappenhagen, granted in personal correspondence

| Sad and angry | Anniversary of my wedding and my divorce several years later. | I believed that I would be married until one of us died. I trusted in his promise. I feel sad for my part in the breakdown of my marriage. I feel sad that we are part of the 50 percent of marriages that fail. I feel angry that everything I tried to do to convince him not to leave failed. I feel sad that he neither forgives me for my part nor recognizes that I was making changes in how I related to him. I feel sad and angry, remembering the betrayal, the shock, the turmoil. I feel sad about my stupidity, my selfishness, and my sin. | I need to put off self-condemnation and keep receiving God's forgiveness. I need to trust in the sovereignty of God that my current life is his will for me. I probably need to pray for my enemy, although I get tired of doing this because I see no indication of change. | "I say to you, love your enemies, bless those who curse you, do good to those who hate you, and pray for those who spitefully use you and persecute you" (Matt. 5:44). "There is therefore now no condemnation to those who are in Christ Jesus" (Rom. 8:1). "Forgive as the Lord forgave you" (Col. 3:13 NIV). "In everything give thanks; for this is the will of God in Christ Jesus for you" (1 Thess. 5:18). |

Feeling	Trigger	Heart demands	Putt off and put on	What God says
Sad, confused, angry, condemned	Being confronted by my good friend over lunch about my responsibility to make sure that my children honor their father.	I was completely unprepared for this criticism, and it hit me out of the blue. Even though I explained my position that because the children are now adults, it is their responsibility to figure out how to honor their father and I do not stand in their way or criticize him, that was not good enough for her. She refused to see him as my enemy—only as the father of my children. It made me question the position I've held all along.	I need to put off her condemnation and rest in my decision to let the children figure out how to honor their father. I'll help them if they ask. I need to pray for him and for the children. I need to take off anger at her for her criticism and allow her to have her own opinion without thinking I have to agree with her or convince her that I am "right." I need to accept her criticism humbly, even if it is unjust. It is a window into my sin that Jesus died for on the cross.	"Bear with each other and forgive whatever grievances you may have against one another. Forgive as the Lord forgave you" (Col. 3:13 NIV).

| Bored with work | Work is uninteresting. I rarely learn anything new. I can do almost everything without a challenge. | I'm tired of doing what I do just because someone needs to do it. After many years, I deserve to have a job that I enjoy. | Put off the false belief that I deserve a job I enjoy. Put on working for the Lord, whatever I do. Put off grumbling and accept my work as a gift from the Lord. And be thankful! | "And do not grumble, as some of them did—and were killed by the destroying angel" (1 Cor. 10:10 NIV). "And whatever you do in word or deed, do all in the name of the Lord Jesus, giving thanks to God the Father through Him" (Col. 3:17). "In everything give thanks, for this is the will of God in Christ Jesus for you" (1 Thess. 5:18). |

Feeling	Trigger	Heart demands	Putt off and put on	What God says
Fear	When I get depressed, then I'm ruled by my fear of being alone, having the responsibility for making my own decisions.	I'm believing a lie that I am alone.	Put off the lie and put on the truth that the Lord is with me. I also need to develop deeper friendships and become part of a community of believers (not just attending church). I was not meant to live as a believer on my own, but in community.	"And I am with you always, even to the very end of the age" (Matt. 28:20).. "Now, therefore, you are no longer strangers and foreigners, but fellow citizens with the saints and members of the household of God, having been built on the foundation of the apostles and prophets, Jesus Christ Himself being the chief cornerstone, in whom the whole building, being fitted together, grows into a holy temple in the Lord, in whom you also are being built together for a dwelling place of God in the Spirit" (Eph. 2:19–22). "I will never leave you nor forsake you" (Heb. 13:5).

| Fear | When someone dies, I feel afraid that I might die soon. My father died when he was still young as did my brother. I may be next. | I deserve to live a long life. | Put off fear and put on trust in God for the days he gives me. Rest in God's great love for me. | "Return to your rest, O my soul, for the LORD has dealt bountifully with you" (Ps. 116:7). "Precious in the sight of the LORD is the death of His saints" (Ps. 116:15). "All the days ordained for me were written in your book before one of them came to be" (Ps. 139:16 NIV). "Are not two sparrows sold for a copper coin? And not one of them falls to the ground apart from your Father's will. But the very hairs of your head are all numbered. Do not fear therefore; you are of more value than many sparrows" (Matt. 10:29–31). "Perfect love casts out fear" (1 John 4:18). |

REFERENCES

AllPsych.com. "Borderline Personality Disorder." 2011. Available at http://allpsych.com/disorders/personality/borderline.html.

Asher, Marshall, and Mary Asher. The Christian's Guide to Psychological Terms. Bemidji, MN: Focus, 2004.

Brandt, Henry, and Kerry Skinner. *The Word for the Wise: Making Scripture the Heart of Your Counseling Ministry.* Nashville: Broadman & Holman, 1995.

Corsini, Raymond J., and Alan J. Auerbach. *Concise Encyclopedia of Psychology.* New York: John Wiley & Sons, Inc., 1998.

The Diagnostic and Statistical Manual of the American Psychiatric Association, Edition IV. Washington, DC: American Psychological Association, 1994.

Driscoll, Mark, and Gerry Breshears. *Death by Love: Letters from the Cross.* Wheaton, IL: Crossway, 2010.

Fitzpatrick, Elyse M., and Jessica Thompson. *Give Them Grace: Dazzling Your Kids with the Love of Jesus.* Wheaton, IL: Crossway, 2011.

Gilbert. Greg. *What Is the Gospel?* Wheaton, IL: Crossway, 2010.

Gillham, Bill. *Lifetime Guarantee: Making Your Christian Life Work and What to Do When It Doesn't.* Brentwood, TN: Wolgemuth & Hyatt, 1987.

Hoffecker, Andrew W., ed. *Revolutions in Worldview: Understanding the Flow of Western Thought.* Phillipsburg, NJ: P&R Publishing, 2007.

Jones, Robert D. *Uprooting Anger: Biblical Help for a Common Problem.* Phillipsburg, NJ: P&R Publishing, 2005.

Kreger, Randi. "Stop Walking on Eggshells: When Someone in Your Life Has Borderline or Narcissistic Personality Disorder." 2011. Available at http://www.psychologytoday.com/blog/stop-walking-eggshells.

Kreisman, Jerold J., and Hal Straus. *I Hate You—Don't Leave Me.* Los Angeles: Body Press, 1989.

Lane, Timothy S., and Paul David Tripp. *How People Change.* Winston-Salem, NC: Punch, 2006.

MacArthur, John, ed. *The MacArthur Study Bible.* Nashville: Thomas Nelson, 1997.

Martin, Enos, and E. A. Vastyan. "Bewildered by the Borderline Personality." *Leadership* (Fall 1989): 42–48.

Masterson, James F. *Psychotherapy of the Borderline Adult: A Developmental Approach.* New York: Brunner/Mazel, 1976.

Miller, Michael. "Borderline Personality Disorder: Origins and Symptoms." *Harvard Mental Health Letter* 22, no. 12 (2006): 1–3.

Moran, Mark. "BPD Researcher Searches for Puzzle's Missing Piece." 2011. Available at http://psychiatryonline.org/newsarticle.aspx?articleid=108570.

———. "Gabbard Weds Neurobiology and Psychodynamics in BPD Treatment." 2011. Available at http://pn.psychiatryonline.org/content/46/7/11.1.full.

———. "Long Journey Led to Advances in Understanding Treatment of Borderline Personality Disorder." 2011. Available at http://psychiatryonline.org/newsarticle.aspx?articleid=108369.

Moskovitz, Richard A. *Lost in the Mirror: An Inside Look at Borderline Personality Disorder.* Dallas: Taylor, 1996.

Needham, David. *Birthright: Christian, Do You Know Who You Are?* Sisters, OR: Multnomah, 1999.

Parker-Pope, Tara. "Coming Out with Mental Illness." 2011. Available at http://well.blogs.nytimes.com/2011/06/23/coming-out-with-mental-illness/?ref=health.

Powlison, David "Cure of Souls (and the Modern Psychotherapies)." *Journal of Biblical Counseling* 25, no. 2 (2007): 29–36.

———. *Power Encounters: Reclaiming Spiritual Warfare.* Grand Rapids: Baker, 1995.

Quick Reference to the Diagnostic Criteria from DSM-IV. Washington, DC: American Psychiatric Association, 1994.

Radmacher, Earl D., Ronald B. Allen, and H. Wayne House, eds. *The Nelson Study Bible.* Nashville: Thomas Nelson, 1997.

Smith, Winston. "Getting the Big Picture of Relationships." *Journal of Biblical Counseling* 22, no. 3 (2004): 2–14.

Tripp, Paul David. *Lost in the Middle: MidLife and the Grace of God.* Wapwallopen, PA: Shepherd Press, 2004.

Welch, Edward T. "Is Biblical-Nouthetic Counseling Legalistic? Reexamination of a Biblical Theme." *Journal of Pastoral Practice* 11, no. 1 (1992): 4–21.

———. "Self-Injury: When Pain Feels Good." *Journal of Biblical Counseling* 22, no. 2 (2004): 31–41.

Wilkerson, Mike. *Redemption: Freed by Jesus from the Idols We Worship and the Wounds We Carry.* Wheaton, IL: Crossway, 2011.

ADDITIONAL RESOURCES

Emotions (e.g., Addictions, Anger, Anxiety, Depression, Panic, Shame, Worry):

Allender, Dan B., and Tremper Longman. *The Cry of the Soul: How Our Emotions Reveal Our Deepest Questions about God.* Colorado Springs: NavPress, 1994.

Anonymous. "Slow Awakening." *Journal of Biblical Counseling* 22, no. 2 (2004): 27–30.

Borgman, Brian S. *Feelings and Faith: Cultivating Godly Emotions in the Christian Life.* Wheaton, IL: Crossway, 2009.

Driscoll, Mark. "Demons Are Tormenting Me" and "He Raped Me." In *Death by Love: Letters from the Cross.* Wheaton, IL: Crossway, 2008.

Emlet, Michael R. "Obsessions and Compulsions: Breaking Free of the Tyranny." *Journal of Biblical Counseling* 22, no. 2 (2004): 15–26.

Farley, William P. "The Poison of Self-Pity." *Journal of Biblical Counseling* 25, no. 3 (2007): 16–11.

Fitzpatrick, Elyse. *Because He Loves Me: How Christ Transforms Our Daily Life.* Wheaton, IL: Crossway, 2010.

Jones, Robert D. "Anger against God." *Journal of Biblical Counseling* 14, no. 3 (1996): 15–20.

———. "Learning Contentment in All Your Circumstances." *Journal of Biblical Counseling* 21, no. 1 (2002): 53–61.

Partain, Melissa. "Sex and Cyberspace." *Journal of Biblical Counseling* 22, no. 1 (2003): 70–80.

Powlison, David. "Anger in Action." *Journal of Biblical Counseling* 25, no. 3 (2007): 6–15.

———. "Predator, Prey and Protector: Helping Victims Think and Act from Psalm 10." *Journal of Biblical Counseling* 16, no. 3 (1998): 27–37.

———. "Sexual Sin and the Wider, Deeper Battles." *Journal of Biblical Counseling* 24, no. 2 (2006): 30–36.

————, ed. "Depression." *Journal of Biblical Counseling* 18, no. 2 (2000): 2–56.

————, ed. "Depression II." *Journal of Biblical Counseling* 18, no. 3 (2000): 2–60.

Sande, Ken. *The Peacemaker: A Biblical Guide to Resolving Personal Conflict.* Grand Rapids: Baker, 1991.

Selle, Andrew H. "The Bridge over Troubled Waters: Overcoming Crippling Fear by Faith and Love," *Journal of Biblical Counseling* 21, no. 1 (2002): 34–40.

Sigler, Chuck. "Panic Attacks: Listen to the Messenger." *Journal of Biblical Counseling* 24, no. 2 (2006): 14–20.

Smith, William P. "Full Disclosure: How God Tells the Story." *Journal of Biblical Counseling* 24, no. 2 (2006): 42–46.

Welch, Edward T. *Addictions: A Banquet in the Grave: Finding Hope in the Power of the Gospel.* Phillipsburg, NJ: P&R Publishing, 2001.

————. "Eating Disorders." *Journal of Biblical Counseling* 24, no. 2 (2006): 9–13.

————. "Exalting Pain? Ignoring Pain? What Do We Do with Suffering?" *Journal of Biblical Counseling* 12, no. 3 (1994): 4–19.

————. "The Madness of Anger." *Journal of Biblical Counseling* 25, no. 3 (2007): 26–35.

————. *When People Are Big and God Is Small.* Phillipsburg, NJ: P&R Publishing, 1997.

Grief and Suffering:

Freeman, Penny N. "An Abuse Survivor Learns to Show Mercy to Her Abuser." *Journal of Biblical Counseling* 21, no. 3 (2003): 42–45.

Miller, Paul E. *A Praying Life: Connecting with God in a Distracting World.* Colorado Springs: NavPress, 2009.

Nicewander, Sue. "I Was in Distress . . . Then I Thought . . ." *Journal of Biblical Counseling* 23, no. 2 (2005): 44–51.

Piper, John. "Counseling with Suffering People." *Journal of Biblical Counseling* 21, no. 2 (2003): 18–27.

Powlison, David, ed. *Journal of Biblical Counseling* 22, no. 1 (2004): 2–57.

———, ed. *Journal of Biblical Counseling* 23, no. 1 (2005): 2–64.

———, ed. *Journal of Biblical Counseling* 25, no. 2 (2007): 2–60.

Tripp, Paul David. "Keeping Destiny in View: Helping Counselees View Life from the Perspective of Psalm 73." *Journal of Biblical Counseling* 13, no. 1 (1994): 13–24.

Helpers' Confidence to Counsel:

Adams, Jay. "Change Them . . . Into What?" *Journal of Biblical Counseling* 13, no. 2 (1995): 13–17.

Boyd, Jeffrey H. "An Insider's Effort to Blow Up Psychiatry." *Journal of Biblical Counseling* 15, no. 3 (1997): 21–31.

Emlet, Michael R. *CrossTalk: Where Life & Scripture Meet.* Greensboro, NC: New Growth Press, 2007.

Lehman, Joseph P. "Believing in Hope: A Meditation on Hope, Expectations and the Nature of Faith." *Journal of Biblical Counseling* 16, no. 2 (1998): 14–23.

Mack, Wayne A. "Developing a Helping Relationship with Counselees." *Journal of Biblical Counseling* 13, no. 1 (1994): 5–12.

Nicewander, Sue. "The Discouraged Counselor." *Journal of Biblical Counseling* 24, no. 2 (2005): 53–57.

Poirer, Alfred J. "Taking Up the Challenge." *Journal of Biblical Counseling* 18, no. 1 (1999): 30–37.

Powlison, David. "The Ambiguously Cured Soul." *Journal of Biblical Counseling* 19, no. 3 (2001): 2–7.

———. "Answers for the Human Condition: Why I Chose Seminary for Training in Counseling." *Journal of Biblical Counseling* 20, no. 1 (2001): 46–54.

———. "The Sufficiency of Scripture to Diagnose and Cure Souls." *Journal of Biblical Counseling* 23, no. 2 (2005): 2–14.

———, ed. *Journal of Biblical Counseling* 25, no. 2 (2007): 2–60.

Schwab, George M., Sr. "The Book of Daniel and the Godly Counselor." *Journal of Biblical Counseling* 14, no. 2 (1996): 32–40.

————. "The Book of Daniel and the Godly Counselor: Part 2." *Journal of Biblical Counseling* 15, no. 1 (1996): 52–61.

Smith, William P. " 'I've Had It with You!' Learning to Be Tender When People Are Tough." *Journal of Biblical Counseling* 22, no. 1 (2003): 31–39.

Tripp, Paul David. *Instruments in the Redeemer's Hands: People in Need of Change Helping People in Need of Change.* Phillipsburg, NJ: P&R Publishing, 2002. Note in particular the appendices, 277–354.

Tripp, Paul David. "Wisdom in Counseling." *Journal of Biblical Counseling* 19, no. 2 (2001): 4–13.

Tyler, David, and Kurt Grady. *Deceptive Diagnosis: When Sin Is Called Sickness.* Bemidji, MN: Focus, 2006.

Welch, Edward T. "Who Are We? Needs, Longings, and the Image of God in Man." *Journal of Biblical Counseling* 13, no. 1 (1994): 25–38.

Motives/Idols:

Going, Lou. "Modern Idolatry: Understanding and Overcoming the Attraction of Your Broken Cisterns." *Journal of Biblical Counseling* 20, no. 3 (2002): 46–52.

Powlison, David. "Idols of the Heart and 'Vanity Fair.' " *Journal of Biblical Counseling* 13, no. 2 (1995): 35–50.

————. "X-ray Questions: Drawing Out the Whys and Wherefores of Human Behavior." *Journal of Biblical Counseling* 18, no. 1 (1999): 2–9.

Welch, Edward T. "Motives: Why Do I Do the Things I Do?" *Journal of Biblical Counseling* 22, no. 1 (2003): 48–56.

Nutrition/Medication:

"Benefits of Folic Acid Proven to Help Depression" and "The Importance of B Vitamins and the Benefits of Folic Acid." *Underground Health Reporter* (2011). Available at http://undergroundhealth reporter.com/benefits-of-folic-acid-helps-depression.

Block, Mary Ann. *Just Because You're Depressed Doesn't Mean You Have Depression.* Hurst, TX: Block System, 2007. See also http://www.blockcenter.com.

"BPD Patients Respond to Omega-3 Fatty Acids." *Psychiatric News* 38, no. 2 (2011). Available at http://psychnews.psychiatryonline .org/newsarticle.aspx?articleid=105646.

Carlat, Daniel. *Unhinged: The Trouble with Psychiatry—A Doctor's Revelations about a Profession in Crisis.* New York: Free Press, 2010.

Citizens Commission on Human Rights International. "CCHR: What We Believe." 2011. Available at http://www.cchr.org/.

"Do Anti-Depressants Work?" *Underground Health Reporter* (2011). Available at http://undergroundhealthreporter.com/do-anti-depressants -work.

Fitzpatrick, Elyse, and Laura Hendrickson. *Will Medicine Stop the Pain? Finding God's Healing for Depression, Anxiety and Other Troubling Emotions.* Chicago: Moody, 2006.

Fredericks, Carlton. *Psycho-Nutrition: A Medical Breakthrough in the Treatment of Mental and Emotional Illness!* New York: Grosset & Dunlap, 1976.

Hoffer, Abram. *Mental Health Regained: 18 Personal Stories of Recovery.* Toronto: International Schizophrenia Foundation, 2007.

Hoffer, Abram, and Andrew W. Saul. *The Vitamin Cure for Alcoholism: How to Protect Against and Fight Alcoholism Using Nutrition and Vitamin Supplementation.* Laguna Beach, CA: Basic Health Publications, 2009.

Kirsch, Irving. *The Emperor's New Drugs: Exploding the Anti-Depressant Myth.* New York: Basic Books, 2010.

McMiller, S. I. *None of These Diseases.* Old Tappan, NJ: Power Books, 1984.

Pfeiffer, Carl C. *Nutrition and Mental Illness: An Orthomolecular Approach to Balancing Body Chemistry.* Rochester, VT: Healing Arts, 1987.

Ross, Julia. *The Mood Cure.* New York: Penguin Books, 2002.

Relationships:

Smith, Winston. "Wisdom in Relationships." *Journal of Biblical Counseling* 19, no. 2 (2001): 32–41.

Secular:

http://www.borderlinepersonalitydisorder.com.

http://www.bpdcentral.org.

Sovereignty:

Adams, Jay E. "Counseling and the Sovereignty of God." *Journal of Biblical Counseling* 11, no. 2 (1993): 4–9.

Bettler, John F. "Jesus' Way of Caring (Mark 4:35–41)." *Journal of Biblical Counseling* 22, no. 1 (2003): 81–84.

Truth, Repentance, Forgiveness, Change:

Lane, Timothy S. "Pursuing and Granting Forgiveness." *Journal of Biblical Counseling* 23, no. 2 (2005): 52–29.

Lane, Timothy S., and Paul David Tripp. "How Christ Changes Us by His Grace." *Journal of Biblical Counseling* 23, no. 2 (2005): 15–21.

Murphy, Tom. "On Prayer: Exodus 33:7–34:10, Matthew 6:5–13." *Biblical Counseling Through Song* (blog). December 7, 2011. Available at http://www.biblicalcounselingthroughsong.org/.

Powlison, David. "Psalm 51: Repenter's Guide." *Journal of Biblical Counseling* 20, no. 1 (2001): 21–39.

Ramsey, D. Patrick. "Judging according to the Bible." *Journal of Biblical Counseling* 21, no. 1 (2002): 62–69.

Sande, Ken. "Judging Others: The Danger of Playing God." *Journal of Biblical Counseling* 21, no. 1 (2002): 12–22.

Smith, William P. "Painstaking Truth for Painful Times." *Journal of Biblical Counseling* 21, no. 1 (2002): 23–33.

Welch, Edward T. "Boundaries in Relationships." *Journal of Biblical Counseling* 22, no. 3 (2004): 15–24.